Schirmer's Visual Libr

Gauguin in Tahiti - The Firs

When the Paris stock exchange crashed in November 1882 a stock-broker by the name of Paul Gauguin (1848–1903) found himself without a living. From the prosperous middle classes he sank "deeper and deeper into the mud" of the proletariat, and was soon only able to offer his wife and five children "dry bread on credit." So he decided to make a career of his passion for painting, and in spring 1891 fled the old world on his own, for the South Sea island of Tahiti.

It was a flight to an exotic paradise, in Gauguin's imagination. But in the late nineteenth century, the unspoiled natural primitiveness Tahiti had once had survived only in areas that resembled reservations, under the rule of French und British colonialists. Gauguin settled in one of the native villages and painted to ward off the disappointment and resignation. The resulting pictures used glowing colors and resplendent surfaces that were less an account of a given reality than the projected dream of a European weary of civilization.

The introduction and commentary on individual paintings in this book are by art historian, writer, and essayist Günter Metken. His study *In Künstlers Lande gehen. Beschreibungen und Essays (The Country of the Artist: Essays)* (ISBN 3-88814-269-5) is available from Schirmer/Mosel.

104 pages, 37 color plates

D1518426

Paul Gauguin about 1891, photographed in Paris by Boutet de Monvel

Gauguin in Tahiti

The First Journey
Paintings 1891–1893

Günter Metken

W. W. Norton
New York   London

Cover painting:
Nafea Faa ipoipo – When will you marry?, 1892
101,5 x 77,5 cm
Rudolf Staechelin Family Foundation, Basel

Translation from German language by Michael Hulse

Reproductions: O.R.T. Kirchner & Graser GmbH, Berlin
Composition: The Sarabande Press, New York
Printed and bound in Germany

ISBN 0-393-30895-2

A Schirmer/Mosel Production
Published by W.W. Norton & Company
New York · London

Contents

The Embarkation for Cythera

Banana tourists. That's what we call passengers who travel to the islands to live at one with Nature, far from the world and free of money worries, eating coconuts and bananas. Take the two Americans travelling with you. They've got just enough money for the crossing. They'll look for a disused native hut and set up home in it, and in a month or so they'll turn up at the police station or their consulate, sick and anaemic, wanting their passage home.

Thus Georges Simenon in his novel *Touristes de bananes* (1937), bringing the dream of Tahiti as an isle of the blessed to a banal and hippie-like conclusion. The book portrays Papeete as a musty French provincial backwater, crawling with whores and as riddled with intrigue as in Gauguin's day. From the very start, Tahiti was the lost paradise par excellence. The end was already contained in its very discovery. Initially, after the Spanish briefly touched land there ("the sailors were given a friendly reception"), it was known in the seventeenth century as Sagittaria. Then in 1767 one Captain Wallis rediscovered the island and, full of English pride of possession, named it after George III. He also, however, stained it with the first blood: fifteen natives lost their lives.

The visit of French explorer Louis-Antoine de Bougainville was a more pleasant one. He arrived half a year later, and recorded the correct name of the island. In 1771 Bougainville published his *Voyage autour du monde,* a book which was widely read, not least for its account of Tahiti as a Garden of Eden and a paradise regained of unconstrained sensuality. As an educator and a nobleman of many parts, Bougainville was wholly natural in his relations with the native people. His report, written from the point of view of an ethnologist and natural scientist, conveys the unfamiliar life and customs of the people, but adds a utopian component to the empirical description; Bougainville, after all, was concerned to place his own culture in a relative light by examining other social structures, thus to establish a tolerant vision of the future drawn from knowledge and experience. He closed his account with a dictionary of the Tahitian language, compiled on the basis of information from Aatourou, who had traveled to Europe with him and died in Madagascar on the return journey.

To the philosophers, Tahiti was long a model of peaceful and carefree communal life as lived before the Fall, before the lust for power and possessions. A myth was born, one which proved as tenacious and delusory as that of the Golden Age.[1] This was what attracted Denis Diderot's criticism. In the very year that the *Voyage autour du monde* was published he wrote a *Supplément au voyage de Bougainville* (though because of its sensitive subject matter it was only circulated in manuscript and not printed till 1796). Like Jean-Jacques Rousseau, Diderot presupposed that humanity in its natural state of liberty, free of social compulsions, was good. European civilization could only ruin that ideal condition—and such ruin, in Diderot's view, was precisely what Bougainville wrought. A Tahitian elder, a family man and a man of honor to suit the taste of a petit bourgeois philosopher, fierily accused the explorer in words fully charged with the dialectic of the Enlightenment:

And you, chief of those robbers who obey you, take ship and leave our shores, and do it fast. We are innocent, we are contented, and you can only harm our happiness. We follow natural instinct in its purity; while you have tried to extinguish its uniqueness in our spirits. Here, every-thing belongs to everyone; but you have preached distinctions of mine and yours and I know not what to us. Our daughters and women belong to us all; you have shared that privilege with us, but you have awoken unfamiliar passions that rage within them. In your arms they became wild; in their arms you became cruel. They began to hate each other; you killed each other on their account, and they returned to us, but stained with your blood. We are free; but you have now planted in our earth the roots of our future enslavement. You are neither a god nor a devil. Who, then, gives you the right to make slaves of others? Leave us our customs; they are more reasonable and more honest than yours. We do not want to exchange what you call our ignorance for your useless knowledge. All that we need and that is good, we already possess. Are we contemptible because we have not succeeded in devising superfluous needs? When we are hungry we have food. When we are cold we have clothing. You have been in our modest homes. What, in your opinion, do they lack? You may take what you call the comforts of life as far as you wish; but permit creatures of reason to stop if the only fruit of continued, toilsome endeavour can be imaginary goods. If you persuade us to cross the cramped confines of mere need, when shall we ever stop working? When shall we be able to enjoy? We have kept the sum of our yearly and daily toil as small as possible because in our view nothing is better than rest. Return to your own country, labour and sweat there as much as you want; but leave us in peace.

Diderot, who was no voyager himself and had never seen the "beautiful people" of the archipelago, was to be proved right in the pessimistic bent of his culture criticism. Certainly the image of Tahiti as an island of love, a new Cythera, has been an enduring one. Right down to Simenon's banana tourists and the Club Méditerranée, now firmly established there, people have gone to Tahiti seeking an El Dorado of the senses, complete with lightly clad playmates offering carefree love. Ever since it was discovered, dropouts of every conceivable kind have gone in pursuit of the chimera seamen spoke of after their lengthy sojourns. Among them were the etcher Charles Meryon and Julien Viaud, who wrote under the pseudonym Pierre Loti, becoming a best-seller of his day and attaining a seat in the Académie Française. Loti's colonial optimism, however sensitively conceived, was well served by the bodies of girls he "married" on a temporary basis, to be used as playthings and pleasures.

In 1879 *Le mariage de Loti* was published, a bittersweet description—a mere hint of rosewater on the leaves of an album, as it were—of the fleeting happiness of a navy lieutenant and thirteen-year-old Rarahu. Gauguin's Teha'amana was the same age. Their life together seems almost to have been anticipated by Loti. Gauguin had devoured the book, probably at the prompting of the well-read van Gogh. In Gauguin's case, of course, everything was more concrete and more brutal. In France in 1894 he told a reporter from the mass-circulation *L'Écho de Paris*: "In order to create anything new, one must seek out the source, the cradle of humanity. The Eve of my choice is still almost animal, and for that reason, despite her nakedness, she is chaste. All the Venuses on show in the Salon here are indecent by comparison, and revoltingly lecherous."

Strindberg and Gauguin

Gauguin's treatment of his child bride resembled the white treatment of the colonies: all condescension, he kept her in dependence. Shockingly egoistic, he sidestepped the European psychological war of the sexes and opted instead for an animal life—this too was an evasion of history. August Strindberg seems to have sensed the contradiction within Gauguin, who was out to liberate Man (in the gender-specific sense) from the bonds of marriage but excluded Woman, as a creature of instinct, from the process, and denied her the right to grow into an adult. The Swedish writer spent the winter of 1894–95 in Paris. His personal life was again in a state of crisis; he spent most of his time in chemical experiments. His recently performed play *The Father* and his study "The Inferiority of Woman to Man," which had been published in the *Revue Blanche,* had put him in the Parisian limelight. The Symbolist circles of writers and artists in which he moved on Montparnasse were the same in which Gauguin, newly returned from Tahiti, moved. The latter instantly recognized the hypersensitive Swede as his own opposite, an independent mind whose judgments were made objectively, from without, rather than on a basis of criteria inherent in art. Gauguin asked Strindberg if he would write a foreword to the catalog of his pictures due for auction at the Hôtel Drouot on February 18, 1895. The writer had no option but to decline. His refusal, though, contained so shrewd a description of Gauguin's haughty individuality (confirmed by adversity) and of his ambiguous Tahitian love that the delighted painter printed it in place of a foreword and added a fictitious reply defending the new paradise and the uncivilized kind of women who lived there—an invented paradise, as Strindberg had acutely noted. The debate between Strindberg and Gauguin goes to the heart of our concerns; it is given here in slightly abridged form:[2]

Strindberg to Gauguin, February 1, 1895
I cannot understand your art and am unable to love it (in particular I have no access at all to your Tahitian art). But I know that this confession will neither surprise nor offend you, since the hatred of others seems mainly to give you strength. Your personality, intent on remaining intact, seems to take pleasure in the aversion it prompts. [. . .]

Yesterday evening I thought of Puvis de Chavannes when, to the southerly sound of mandolin and guitar, I saw the sunny pictures hanging higgledy-piggledy on your studio walls. They pursued me in my sleep last night. I saw trees that no botanist would recognize, animals whose existence was unsuspected by Cuvier, and people only you could have created. A sea that seemed to have flowed from a volcano, and heavens no god could inhabit. My dear sir (I told myself in a dream), you have created a new heaven and earth, but I do not like it in your creation. For me, a lover of chiaroscuro, it is too sunny. And in your paradise lives an Eve who is not my ideal, for I do have one or two ideals of woman of my own.[. . .]

No, Gauguin was not fashioned from Chavanne's rib, nor from Manet's or Bastien Lepage's. But who is he? He is Gauguin, the savage, who detests tedious civilization; a Titan who, in his envy of the Creator, uses his leisure to produce a creation of his own in miniature; a child taking his toys apart and making new ones of them. Who denies and defies. Who would rather see the sky as red than blue as the multitude see it.

Gauguin to Strindberg, February 5, 1895

Today I received your letter, a foreword for my catalog. The thought of asking you for this foreword came to me one evening recently when I saw you playing the guitar and singing in my studio. Your blue Nordic eyes were fixed attentively on the pictures hanging on the walls. I had a premonition of revolt, of a proper clash between your civilization and my barbarism: the civilization under which you suffer, the barbarism which makes a new man of me.

When you saw the Eve I prefer, painted in the shapes and harmonies of another world, you will perhaps have recalled a painful past of your own. The Eve of your civilized imagination makes you and almost all of us misogynists; the Eve of primitive times who, in my studio, startles you now, may one day smile on you less bitterly.[. . .]

The Eve I have painted—and she alone—can remain naturally naked before us. Yours, in this simple state, could not move without a feeling of shame, and too beautiful, perhaps, would provoke misfortune and suffering.

To make my line of thought more comprehensible to you, let me compare, instead of the two women, the Maori language of my Eve with the inflected, European language of your chosen one.

In the Oceanic languages, which are limited to essential constituents preserved in a raw state and either standing alone or juxtaposed crudely and without any thought of polish, everything is still naked and unspoiled. By contrast, in your inflected languages the roots in which they, like all languages, had their origins are obscured by daily usage which wears away the relief and contours. It is a fine mosaic, and one no longer notices the crudeness with which the pieces may be joined together but rather merely admires a beautiful image made of stones. Only a practiced eye can identify the way the thing is made.

Forgive this lengthy philosophical digression. I felt it was necessary in order to explain the crude art I use to adorn that land and its people.

Murnau and Matisse, or, A Farewell to Exoticism

Common to all the reports of Tahiti is the quest for simple, primitive naturalness. To want to recover that state is sheer wishful thinking. Those who beheld it at first hand, such as Cook, Bougainville, and Forster, were to a greater or lesser extent seeing partially (in both senses). And those who set out to apprehend it at a later date found it gone forever. This is the paradoxical fate of the ethnologist, identified by Lévi-Strauss in *Tristes Tropiques*. And this is why people tried time and again to reconstruct the lost paradise.

One last attempt was made by the German film director Friedrich Wilhelm Murnau in his film *Taboo,* on which Robert O'Flaherty collaborated. Arriving by yacht from California, he spent 1929–30 in the archipelago, with the Southern Cross constantly before his eyes: "Soon, once we have the Equator behind us, it will outshine all the books and dreams," wrote Murnau — "after all, we are pursuing the books and dreams."[3] It could not be put more clearly. Murnau reached the craggy island of Nuku-Hiva in the Marquesas, described by Herman Melville in *Typee,* "captivated by the beauty of these people, their ideal physique, their courtesy and hospitality, the unbroken atmosphere of good cheer; supposedly they have known neither hunger nor sickness nor fear."

In place of reed-thatch huts he found European-style houses. But the magic of the South Seas remained, albeit with a touch of nostalgia and retrospection:

> There was the beach of white sand, the tall slender coconut palms, the bushes with their fantastic red blooms and the trees with their white frangipani flowers like alabaster, the scent wafted about the island on the gentle breeze. Away beyond all the splendor rise the mountains; we could see wild goats grazing on those steep heights. The mountains seemed to lend a forbidding note to that paradise. Cleft and craggy, they towered to the clouds, reminiscent of angry gods left to die by a whole tribe of humanity.

Brown-skinned natives, some of whom were splendidly built, rowed up to our boat in their trimarans.[. . .] They merely looked at us in silence—from their lips neither laughter nor song was to be heard. We went ashore in the noonday heat. From the *burao* trees, large yellow blossoms fluttered to earth. Thus—we thought with involuntary despondency—has the flower of this once great race fallen into oblivion. It was not an encouraging reflection, given that we had come a full 4,000 miles to capture for the screen these last fading rays of a destroyed splendor. We realized that it would take time, persistence, love, hard work and research to re-create the image of paradise presented to the world by Melville, Stevenson and O'Brien. Although our destination was Tahiti, about 1,000 miles distant, we decided to investigate every bay and valley of the Marquesas, in the hope of finding people who still possessed something of the pride and beauty and spirit of their fore-bears. And they would take the main parts in the film we had come to make.[4]

To re-create the image of paradise, and erase the white discovery from history, was the driving impulse behind this argonautic voyage, with Gauguin as pilot. Murnau reports that, when they heard grammophone music in the house of a European, the people of Uda-Pu, whom missionaries had forbidden to dance, began "a wild dance, moving their bodies rhyth-mically. It was as if Gauguin's pictures had come to life." One painting, *The Spirit of the Dead Keeps Watch,* inspired the scene in *Taboo* "where Reri the native woman is lying on her flat bed undecided whether she really did see her pursuer, a Tahitian Nosferatu, wielding a harpoon instead of a scythe, or whether her fears were playing visual tricks on her. The film audience is in the same dilemma. Fear cannot be conveyed in visual images with any greater realism than through visions."[5]

That year of 1930 was conceivably a turning point in the way Tahiti was seen and prized. The myth, recalled to life one more time in the film, faded forever. Henri Matisse, who was there at the same time as Murnau and was photographed by the director beneath palm trees,[6] was disappointed by the island, as an artist; that *aetas aurea* he aimed at in his paintings already existed, leaving him nothing more to do. The natural life of the tropics struck him as lush but prompted no enthusiasm in him; he thought it "domestic luxuriance," instantly familiar. The trees looked like "indoor plants." He missed resistance, missed creative tension: "On Tahiti I could appreciate the light, light as a pure substance, and the coral earth. It is at once a magnificent and a boring land. It knows nothing of the worries we have from our early youth on and which probably help keep us alive. There, the weather is beautiful from sunrise and remains unchanged till evening. Bliss so uniform is wearying."[7]

Not until the 1940s did his Tahiti experience of brightness and clear domestic shapes enter Matisse's works, in his cutouts and his decor for the chapel at Vence.

And what of Gauguin?

"Gauguin went there as a rebel. That kept him going in an environment that turns one to wood, as they say there. His contentious character, his life as a crucified man, saved him from the all-pervasive somnolence. His hurt self-love kept him awake."[8]

For Matisse, the journey to Tahiti via New York constituted a farewell to Gauguin, whose colors and hedonistic subjects had so long been his constant companion. Now he needed a greater sense of space, in his book illustrations and in the decorative work of his late period: "I was not thinking of Gauguin, and when I did suppose I had come across him, in a remote district, in front of a cottage and its inhabitants wearing *paréos*, I set aside everything I had loved in Gauguin and his art as old-fashioned junk."[9]

It was the end of the picturesque. A farewell to exoticism.

Gauguin's Tahiti: The Dream and the Reality

For Gauguin, on the other hand, everything initially seemed unambiguous. He had gone "as a rebel." Repelled by the supposed decadence and hypocritical morality of Europe, the artist set out in quest of purity and truth. He thought he would find them in remote regions such as Brittany, with its peasant ways, Celtic language, and purifying sea. This was a prevalent topos at the turn of the century, from Strindberg to Debussy and Böcklin. But in

Brittany, too, Paris and art dealing and Christendom (to which he wished to oppose an art both virgin and sanctified) proved omnipresent. Gauguin therefore turned to archaic cultures and peoples who were thought to be "natural," and made their charisma of primitiveness as much his own as he did the statuary of ancient India. What resulted was an art of the perpetual present, or of eternal recurrence. Beautiful creatures entirely at their ease are seen inhabiting the tropical garden. Whenever the rapprochement of the world's different cultures, the fertilization of our own art by other ethnographic models, or primitivism, have been debated since, Paul Gauguin has been seen as the star witness.[10] Yet there can be no question of a straight, linear aesthetic evolution in his work. Rather, it is a thing of amalgamation, projection, and dream images.

After a voyage of two months, Gauguin had Tahiti before his eyes on June 9, 1891. What was it that he saw? Not the untouched island he had hoped for, but a French protectorate divided up into administrative districts, with gendarmes, schoolteachers, missionaries. The main town, Papeete, where arrivals disembarked, had a population of three thousand. A few dozen officials from the mother country, changed every three years, occupied the key positions. They remained in their *cercles,* with a minimum of contact with the two hundred or so French settlers who had remained after completing military service, married native women, and gone into wholesale or retail trade, opening shops or cafés. There were three hundred planters and merchants of British origin too, viewed with suspicion by the French and shunned socially by all, yet omnipresent. There were also the same number of Chinese. And finally, the largest ethnic group but with the smallest influence, there were two thousand Tahitians.

Arrogance and envy, resentment and quarrels prevailed among these groupings. Furthermore, there were religious rivalries. The French were Catholic, the Tahitians predominantly Protestant; both communities sought to convert the other, a kind of religious war which educated persons found distasteful. No wonder that Gauguin was deeply disappointed on finding, at the other end of the world, another Europe—"the Europe which I had thought to shake off—and that under the aggravating circumstances of colonial snobbism, and the imitation, grotesque even to the point of caricature, of our customs, fashions, vices, and absurdities of civilization. Was I to have made this far journey, only to find the very thing which I had fled?"

But for the company of a few understanding colonists, among them Lieutenant Jénot, Gauguin was largely on his own. So-called society, once word of his alcoholic indulgences and lack of funds got around, dropped him once the initial protection of official introductions had worn off. Gauguin left Papeete for Mataiea, forty-six kilometers to the south, where he moved into a hut. But there too he found no seclusion. For that, he was a century too late. Or else he should have chosen a less Europeanized island with an intact population, as Robert Louis Stevenson did when he retired to Samoa and died there. Henry Adams and John La Farge visited him and witnessed the simplicity of his life. For the South Seas at the close of the nineteenth century, as the writings of Joseph Conrad, Stevenson, and Somerset Maugham show, were a refuge for those who were tired of civilization, who were suffering what Freud termed its discontents.

Tahiti, however beautiful it might be, was no longer that kind of refuge. It consisted largely of mountains rising inaccessibly to heights of two thousand meters, so that settlements were confined to the narrow coastal strip where roads were feasible. Alcohol and introduced diseases had had a devastating effect on the population: from 150,000 before the discovery, it had dwindled to 15,000. People subsisted on a pig or two, chickens and dogs (considered a delicacy), and lived on a mainly vegetarian diet of bananas, oranges, guavas, mangoes, coconuts, and the fruits of the pandanus and breadfruit trees, all provided in abundance by a profligate nature. Outside the town, food and money worries were almost unknown. Ambition, rivalry, and the need to work were even less familiar, with the result that the people were open and hospitable, taking pleasure in music, dancing, and games. Rest, bathing, and love were their innocent amusements.

It was this atmosphere, albeit sullied by missions of the two principal Christian denominations, that Gauguin found at Mataiea. Delighted by the colorfulness and freshness of his new surroundings, he set to work. By Christmas 1891 he had painted some twenty pictures that reflected his new acquaintance with the natural native people and their world. They were people who suited his artistic ideal of a single-minded solemnity à la Puvis de

Chavannes: they could remain at rest for hours, daydreaming or dozing, in a relaxed attitude that seemed contemplative. At that time, Gauguin aphoristically advised prospective artists: "All things should breathe calm and peace of spirit. For this reason movement should be avoided. Every one of the figures should be in a static condition."

But the initial magic spell did not hold for long. For one who made Gauguin's demands and had Gauguin's aversion to civilization, everyday life on Tahiti was rather a disappointment. He was also in urgent need of money, putting everything on credit with the Chinese; and when, naively overestimating his suitability, he applied for the job of justice of the peace, he was rejected by the governor of the island. Gauguin was now compelled to tighten his belt and live without alcohol or tobacco. He wrote to Europe requesting advances; but replies from Europe took four months, which meant an enervating wait for the monthly mail packet while he lived on the credit and generosity of a handful of acquaintances. To keep himself busy (he was not always in a frame of mind to work) he immersed himself in writings on old Polynesian culture, of which little or nothing remained on Tahiti. He read a disquisition on Tahiti published in 1855 by a naval officer, Edmond de Bovis, and more particularly the two-volume *Voyage aux îles du Grand Océan* (1832) by Jacques-Antoine Moerenhout, which conveyed the old Maori civilizations through narratives, without imposing the author's worldview but nonetheless with poetic fire. Both works were relatively imprecise compared with English sources such as Captain Cook's report or the *Polynesian Researches* (1827) of William Ellis, a missionary; but Gauguin did not have the English to read these. Nor did our outsider come across Arii Taimai, an old aristocratic native who presented Maori songs and legends in Papeete at that time. In any case he understood too little Tahitian. He began eagerly to acquire scraps of the melodious language, which had few consonants and always ended on vowel sounds; and these he used as keys to his paintings.

His new companion Teha'amana introduced him more directly to the language and customs of the archipelago. Following Pierre Loti's example and the coupling that was normal on the island, Gauguin had sealed a Polynesian marriage: that is, he had taken a thirteen-year-old girl in exchange for gifts to her parents, real and adoptive. We know what Teha'amana

Teha'amana, about 1894.
Photographer unknown

looked like from the pictures that he now painted in large number once again. And their life together is seen through rose-tinted spectacles in *Noa Noa*:

> Then a life filled to the full with happiness began. Happiness and work rose up together with the sun, radiant like it. The gold of Tehura's face flooded the interior of our hut and the landscape round about with joy and light. She no longer studied me, and I no longer studied her. She no longer concealed her love from me, and I no longer spoke to her of my love. We lived, both of us, in perfect simplicity. How good it was in the morning to seek refreshment in the nearest brook, as did, I imagine, the first man and the first woman in Paradise. Tahitian paradise, *nave nave fenua*—land of delights!
>
> And the Eve of this paradise became more and more docile, more loving. I was permeated with her fragrance—*noa noa*. She came into my life at the perfect hour. Earlier, I might, perhaps, not have understood her, and later it would have been too late. Today 1 understand how much I love her, and through her I enter into mysteries which hitherto remained inaccessible to me.[11]

Hina and Fatu, about 1892
Tamanu-Wood
height 32.7 cm, diameter 14.2 cm
Art Gallery of Ontario

Teha'amana did the cooking, laundry, and shopping while "Koke" (as his name was rendered by the Tahitians) was at his work. She also had other lovers — the other side of sexual liberty. Through her, Gauguin acquired a better grasp of the local mentality, and now started to idealize all things Tahitian, including the past, which he invoked using carved idols. These were unrelated to contemporary Tahitian art, which in Gauguin's day no longer presented gods or ancestors but merely crude, anthropomorphic, bulky sculptures. Gauguin's idols were composite recollections of the immense Easter Island figures, statues of the Buddha, Egyptian Pharaohs, and Indian reliefs.

By the end of 1892, the charms of Tahiti and of the fickle Teha'amana interested him no more. Gauguin had painted fifty pictures and considered his mission accomplished. Moreover, a large-scale joint exhibition with van Gogh was being organized in Copenhagen, which (in the eyes of his family there) would cleanse him of the stigma of parasitism. But, penniless as he was, his return was delayed until the government, seeing him as a "needy artist," granted him free passage. In late May he set off, and on August 1, 1893, he arrived in Marseilles — without a sou — where he waited till friends lent him the train fare to Paris.

Of Gauguin's troubled financial status, the constant defeats of the social outcast, and the wretched and humiliating life (despite everything) which he led in the colonies, his pictures tell us nothing. Was he too proud to concede failure? Or was he too much the artist? The paintings almost exclusively show young, beautiful people in a realm of perpetual peace. They are pictures of paradise, icons of the Golden Age. We recall how Dostoyevsky unmasked his arcadian world as a retreat from the here and now:

> In the Dresden gallery hangs a painting by Claude Lorrain which the catalog identifies as *Acis and Galatea* — I have always thought of it as *The Golden Age*. In that picture, mankind in Europe recorded its memory of the cradle, and the thought of it fills my soul with something like homesickness. At one time it was an earthly paradise for humanity: the gods descended from heaven and were kin to mankind. Oh, they were beautiful people who lived there. Happy and guiltless they woke and slept. The groves and meadows were filled with their songs and rejoicing. The great superabundance of vital powers issued in love and pure pleasure. The sun bathed them in warmth and light and delighted in their beautiful children. What a wonderful dream! What a sublime human aberration! Of all the illusions mankind has ever cherished, the Golden Age is the least probable" (*The Raw Youth,* 1875).

The Garden of Eden as Private Mythology

Gauguin was by no means original in going to Tahiti. Many had preceded him to the new Cythera. Even in Goethe's Germany there were those who wanted to drop out, and among nineteenth-century French intellectuals — Delacroix, Meryon, Baudelaire, Rimbaud, Flaubert, Loti, to name just a few — there was a regular exodus to the Orient and the Society Islands. People were well informed — by the colonial office and by the findings of a diligent ethnological discipline still in its infancy — concerning Tahiti and the archipelago. Essentially Gauguin opted for a literary topos; he was succumbing to an evocative name which, ever since Bougainville, had promised love and carefree work, and pleasures without remorse in a paradisical setting.

Genuinely primitive, less garden-like regions would scarcely have been suitable for this.

The reason why Gauguin was at odds with contemporary reality, and always found his Edens already profaned, may lie in his own personality and origins. He liked to see himself as an exile without roots, a wanderer—even in the famous self-portrait *Bonjour, Monsieur Gauguin* in Prague. The son of a journalist veteran of 1848, he was also the grandson of Flora Tristan, the early socialist writer, who in turn was the illegitimate daughter of a Peruvian general and called herself "Paria." Gauguin initially grew up in Lima, in the care of a black nanny and a Chinese servant. He always liked to highlight the "Indian" streak in himself and his supposedly Inca profile. As a young man he spent several years sailing around the world in the navy, first as a cadet and then in military service.

The period that followed was almost one of middle-class normality. He married Mette Gad, a staunchly Protestant Danish woman, and made a successful career in business. He was also successful as an amateur painter and made contact with the impressionists, exhibiting with them from 1879 to 1886. Pissarro introduced him to *plein air* painting. Edgar Degas, to whom he owed much formally, supported him. When in 1883 he found himself on the street following a stock exchange collapse, Gauguin chose to become an artist and, after a depressing stay in Copenhagen, separated from his wife and children, who remained in Denmark. Socially an outcast and "halfbreed," Gauguin cultivated the image of Flying Dutchman through his ostentation and his escapes—to Brittany, to the Caribbean, to Tahiti, and finally to the Marquesas, fifteen hundred kilometers farther on in the nowhere of the ocean. Led on by an indefinable longing for the primitive and natural, he was most assuredly not seeking an intact and unspoiled society in the ethnologist's sense, but rather a private Eden amid lush nature, the finest fruits of which were brown-skinned girls. On civilized Tahiti, Gauguin had no option but to invent a paradise of his own, which he then furnished with a private mythology of his own, painting, carving, producing decorative art, and even inventing a dark goddess of his own, Oviri, the savage one. Gauguin's island was largely an imaginary thing, a world of will and idea. It was also biographically encoded, full of personal obessions.

When in 1893 he returned to France for a good eighteen months, he wrote an illustrated volume intended as an explanatory supplement to the paintings he had brought with him: *Noa Noa* (i.e. Fragrance). This account, which emphasized harmony and was interspersed with traditional Maori beliefs he had read of or intuitively grasped, had little or nothing to do with Gauguin's real life on Tahiti. He was creating his own legend, making a symbolist program for his art: at the time he was patently out to be the aesthetic leader of the writes and critics grouped about Stéphane Mallarmé, by whom he felt himself to be understood. Gauguin superimposed on the beautiful people of Tahiti, robbed of their roots by the brainwashing of colonial rule, his own exoticism and the syncretistic culture of the autodidact bent on blending the traditions of Europe, Asia, ancient America, and Polynesia. He had in mind an overriding musical rhythm of form and color. Solid shapes borrowed from sculpture were composed in plastic groups, flatteringly enhanced by patterned fabrics and by the sweeping contours of waves, mountains, trees, leaves, and beaches, in such a way that — as it were — emblematic representations of the Golden Age resulted. The still lifes of firm and luscious fruits and vessels echoed these.

These pastorals please our eyes and senses but emanate no happiness of their own. It is not only that Gauguin repeatedly brings on the ghosts of the dead to torment the living through nightmares — which at that point was evidently the sole remaining religious tenet in which he firmly believed. None of his Tahitian women are seen smiling, either: every one of them is melancholy. This may be a product of the seriousness prevalent in symbolism, of its horror of the anecdotal. But Gauguin was also trying to convey something enigmatic in their dark eyes and averted faces, to record a mystery. *Soyez mystérieuses — soyez amoureuses* was his message in an age stripped of magic. The fact that such an appeal needed to be made indicates how far removed he felt himself to be from any such mystery. But the immobility of the faces, rendered as wonderful masks in exquisite draftsmanship, also testifies to the unbridgeable divide between alien cultures and races. Matisse was surely right: it was only in a position of conflict, as one who suffered among others who were unreflectingly happy, that Gauguin could create his artistic paradise.

Notes

1. Cf. *Mythos Tahiti. Südsee—Traum und Realität,* catalog of the exhibition at the Stuttgart Linden-Museum, Berlin, 1987.
2. Translated from Françoise Cachin: *Gauguin, "ce malgré moi de sauvage,"* Paris, 1989, pp. 166–69.
3. Translated from Lotte H. Eisner: *Murnau, der Klassiker des deutschen Films* Hannover, 1967, p. 110.
4. Ibid., pp. 110–11·
5. Translated from Frieda Grafe, "Dem German Genius: Friedrich Wilhelm Murnau zum 100. Geburtstag," *Die Zeit* no. 51 (December 16, 1988), p. 60. My thanks to the author for checking this again at the cutting table.
6. Reproduced in Alfred H. Barr, Jr., *Matisse, His Art and His Public* (New York, 1951) (1968 reprint), p. 28.
7. Translated from *Matisse et Tahiti,* Cahiers Henri Matisse I (Nice: Musée Matisse, 1986), p. 28.
8. Ibid., p. 32.
9. Ibid., p. 36.
10. Cf. the exhibition catalog *Weltkulturen und moderne Kunst,* Munich, 1972; *Primitivism in 20th Century Art,* New York, 1984; *Exotische Welten—europäische Phantasien,* Stuttgart, 1987.
11. Paul Gauguin: *Noa Noa,* translated from the French by O. F. Theis (New York, 1919) (1985 reprint), p. 32.

Plates

All of the paintings reproduced here were done in oil
on canvases of varying textures.

1   *Self-Portrait with Idol*   1891
46 x 33 cm
Marion Koogler McNay Institute, San Antonio (Texas)

This portrait was one of the first pictures Gauguin painted on Tahiti. In *Noa Noa* he wrote:

"In order to familiarize myself with the distinctive characteristics of the Tahitian face, I had wished for a long time to make a portrait of one of my neighbours, a young woman of pure Tahitian extraction.

"One day she finally became emboldened enough to enter my hut, and to look at photographs of paintings which I had hung on one of the walls of my room.[. . .]

"While she was curiously examining certain religious compositions of the Italian primitives, I hastened, without her noticing it, to sketch her portrait.

"She saw it, and with a pout cried out abruptly, *'Aïta!'* (no) and fled.

"An hour later she returned, dressed in a beautiful robe with the *tiaré* behind the ear. Was it coquetry? Was it the pleasure of consenting of her own free will after having refused? Or was it simply the universal attraction of the forbidden fruit which one denies one's self? Or more probably still, was it merely a caprice without any other motive, a pure caprice of the kind to which the Maoris are so given?

"Without delay I began work, without hesitation and all of a fever. I was aware that on my skill as painter would depend the physical and moral possession of the model, that it would be like an implied, urgent, irresistible invitation.

"She was not at all handsome according to our aesthetic rules.

"She was beautiful.

"All her traits combined in a Raphaelesque harmony by the meeting of curves. Her mouth had been modelled by a sculptor who knew how to put into a single mobile line a mingling of all joy and all suffering."

2   *Vahine no te Tiare (Woman with a Flower)*   1891

70 x 46 cm

Ny Carlsberg Glyptotek, Copenhagen

P art still life and part genre painting, this picture is unique in Gauguin's work of the period. The gaze of the boy on the right, the phallic shapes of the bananas, and the symbolism of the bowls have prompted interpretation in terms of awakening sexuality. But Gauguin seems to have arranged the fruits and vessels on the table (which a Tahitian household does not have) mainly for their color values.

The red bananas are considered a delicacy on Tahiti, though they can only be eaten cooked. The frieze behind the youngsters — who may simply be feeling intimidated by the foreign painter — attests to Gauguin's growing interest in decorative art. The fruits and utensils cast hard-defined shadows, unlike the people, who may have been added to the finished still life as an afterthought.

3   *The Meal*   1891

73 × 92 cm

Musée d'Orsay, Paris

"We found them indeed to answer the expectations we had formed of a country described as an elysium by M. de Bougainville. We entered a grove of breadfruits, on most of which we saw no fruit at this season of winter, and followed a neat but narrow path, which led to different habitations, half hid under various bushes. Tall coco-palms nodded to each other, and rose over the rest of the trees; the bananas displayed their beautiful large leaves, and now and then one of them still appeared loaded with its clustering fruit. A sort of shady trees, covered with a dark-green foliage, bore golden apples, which resembled the anana in juiciness and flavour. Betwixt these the intermediate space was filled with young mulberry-trees (*morus papyrifera*) of which the bark is employed by the natives in the manufacture of their cloth; with several species of arum or eddies, with yams, sugar-canes, and other useful plants."

George Forster, *A Voyage round the World*, 1777

4   *Te ra'au rahi (The Big Tree)*   1891

73 X 91.5 cm

Art Institute of Chicago

"We found the cottages of the natives scattered at short distances, in the shade of fruit-trees, and surrounded by various odoriferous shrubs, such as the gardenia, guettarda, and calophyllum. The neat simplicity of their structure gave us no less pleasure than the artless beauty of the grove which encompassed them. The pandang or palm-nut tree had given its long prickly leaves to thatch the roofs of the buildings, and these were supported by a few pillars made of the bread-tree, which is thus useful in more respects than one. As a roof is sufficient to shelter the natives from rains and nightly dews, and as the climate of this island is perhaps one of the happiest in the world, the houses seldom have any walls, but are open to all sides. We saw, however, a few dwellings constructed for greater privacy, which were entirely enclosed in walls of reeds, connected together by transverse pieces of wood, so as to give us the idea of large bird-cages. In these there was commonly a hole left for the entrance, which could be closed up with a board. Before every hut, on the green turf or on dry grass, we observed groups of inhabitants lying down or sitting in the eastern style, and passing their happy hours away in conversation or repose."

George Forster, *A Voyage round the World*, 1777

5   *Te ra'au rahi (The Big Tree)*   1891

74 x 92.8 cm

Cleveland Museum of Art

At first Gauguin tirelessly investigated his new chosen home. In this picture, the animals, the house gables, the trees, and the outlines of the hills are all still reminiscent of Brittany. The use of color continues from the Martinique landscapes.

6 *Haere mai* 1891

74 x 92 cm

Solomon R. Guggenheim Museum, New York

*P*aysage Papeete was Gauguin's title for this work in a list drawn up early in 1892. The trodden earth path and low rampart at left are characteristic of the Papeete region. The woman squatting at right is in the same position as Teha'amana in *Te faaturuma,* suggesting that this might be Gauguin's own hut at Mateiea or that of his companion at Papeete. The spatial perspective, leading towards the mountains, is unlike the flat, carpet effect of other landscapes done at this time.

7　*Village Street on Tahiti*　1891

117 x 89 cm

Museum of Art, Toledo (Ohio)

This is the only picture of expressly Christian content painted during the first Tahiti sojourn. Gauguin thought it of great importance, and the Paris press in 1893 hailed it as a modern master-piece. In a letter of March 11, 1892, to Daniel de Monfreid, Gauguin described it in these terms: "An angel with yellow wings is showing us two Tahitian women, Mary, and Jesus, these last also Tahitian. They are unclothed but for their *paréos* of flowered cotton loosely fastened at the waist. Beyond there are very dark mountains and trees in blossom. A dark violet path and emerald green foreground. I am most satisfied."

Since Gauguin was primarily interested in subjects drawn from Maori mythology at the time, it has been supposed that *Ia orana Maria* was painted to mark his recovery from hepatitis, which had necessi-tated a lengthy stay in hospital.

The iconography departs from Christian tradition. The infant Jesus is not present at the annunciation. The resplendently colored angel, conceived after Botticelli, holds the palm of martyrdom—a serious note in this earthly paradise embracing the bounty of nature and the peace of the village community. The two women coming in adoration were inspired by a frieze on Borobudur (eighth/ninth century), the Buddhist monument on Java. Thus Europe, Asia, and Polynesia meet in this painting.

IA ORANA MARIA

8 *Ia orana Maria (Hail Mary)* 1891

113.7 x 87.6 cm

Metropolitan Museum of Art, New York

In *Noa Noa* Gauguin gave a poetic description of the view from his hut at Mataiea:

"On the sea close to the strand I see a pirogue, and in the pirogue a half-naked woman. On the shore is a man, also undressed. Beside the man is a diseased coconut tree with shriveled leaves. It resembles a huge parrot with golden tails hanging down, and holding in his claws a huge cluster of coconuts. With a harmonious gesture the man raises a heavy axe in his two hands. It leaves above a blue impression against the silvery sky, and below a rosy incision in the dead tree, where for an inflammatory moment the ardour stored up day by day throughout centuries will come to life again."

9   *Man with an Ax*   1891

92 x 70 cm

Private collection, Switzerland

Europeans were always fascinated by the Tahitian women's practice of bathing naked and at great leisure. Writers of the Enlightenment saw it as striving for purity and physical vigor in a wearing climate. On the other hand, the brown-skinned naiads made a distinctly erotic impression on French sailors, as George Forster observed:

"The simplicity of a dress which exposed to view a well proportioned bosom and delicate hands, might also contribute to fan their amorous fire; and the view of several of these nymphs swimming nimbly all round the sloop, such as nature had formed them, was perhaps more than sufficient entirely to subvert the little reason which a mariner might have left to govern his passions."

A good hundred years later, Pierre Loti remarked that his Tahitian partner Rarahu's main pastimes were daydreaming and bathing, "above all bathing." Nymphs taking a carefree dip in all their divine innocence are staples of the Golden Age, the fading image of which Gauguin was seeking on Tahiti. In Brittany he had already been arrested by the motif of well-made figures seen from the rear as they plunge naked into the waves. In this picture, everything makes a more tranquil, arabesque impression, including the shore in the foreground, which looks like a textile design and echoes the printed fabric of the girl on the right, just as the blossoms and the crests of waves echo each other. Initially Gauguin would sketch out such compositions as a network of wavy lines, which he then colored in. To heighten the luminous force of the colors he glazed them with a thin coating of wax.

Fatata te Miti (written on painting, lower left)

P. Gauguin (signature, lower right)

10   *Fatata te Miti (Near the Sea)*   1892
67.9 x 91.5 cm
National Gallery of Art, Washington

Two women sitting nonchalantly on the floor, doubtless painted from the same model, Teha'amana. Their contours are counterpoised yet interlinked. The bright colors of their *paréos* correspond and echo. The close-up creates an unusual monumentality in this still life of bodies, which is perhaps not set on a beach before the green waves of the sea, as generally assumed, but on a terrace, one wooden post of which can be seen in the background at top right. Everything is motionless except for the eyes of the woman on the right, who is perhaps reacting to the news expressed in the title. Gauguin was forever concerned to involve these sculpturally conceived figures in taut colouring and a construct of plane and surface.

11   *Parau Api? (What's new? — Two Tahitian Women)*   1892

67 x 92 cm

Gemäldegalerie Neue Meister, Dresden

At first Gauguin insisted on giving his pictures only Tahitian titles—which did not exactly help sales. This title, he said, meant silence or a brooding mood. And indeed, the girl so lost in her own thoughts does seem to convey the oppressive silence of the island and its people, which all the travelers reported. Gauguin too, shortly after his arrival, tried to describe it in a letter to his wife: "Always this quiet. I now understand how these people can sit for hours and days without saying a word, gazing sadly at the sky."

In November 1893, after being exhibited at Durand-Ruel's, *Te faaturuma* was bought by Edgar Degas, whose own resting dancers had plainly inspired the position the girl is seen in. There may also be an allusion to a ritual posture of the Buddha. The cigarlike object is perhaps being burned to keep off insects. The house is in colonial style, and the young woman may possibly be brooding upon the horseman outside the veranda.

12   *Te faaturuma (Brooding Woman)*   1891

91.2 x 68.7 cm

Worcester Art Museum, Worcester (Mass.)

This was doubtless one of the first of twenty pictures Gauguin painted in late 1891 when he had left Papeete and rented the hut at Mataiea. The picture at top left, no longer traceable, probably shows the bamboo hut he was living in there. His furniture included this rocking chair brought from Papeete. The chair, the muted colors, and the ankle-length mission dress covering the entire body make this full-length portrait of a young Tahitian woman relatively European in appearance. The melancholy of the model with face averted, who has been taken for Teha'amana, represented the unfathomable mystery of an alien race for Gauguin.

13   *Faaturuma (Melancholy)*   1891

94.6 x 68.8 cm

The Nelson Atkins Museum of Art, Kansas City (Mo.)

Three-quarter portrait of Teha'amana in a violet Sunday dress. Her loosened hair with white gardenias (*tiaré*) in it, and the mango in her hand, render her an Oceanic Eve, her dark fiery eyes and sensual mouth confirming her as the very personification of seduction. Teha'amana's ample proportions are those of a pregnant woman. "In Oceania I shall soon be a father again," Gauguin wrote to Daniel de Monfreid in August 1892—a prospect which turned out to be unfounded in this case.

The head, shoulders, and arms of this woman with gaze mysteriously averted stand out sharply against the chrome yellow background. While that background and the flower-pattern blue material suggest an interior, the fruit seems to have been picked from the tree at top left; but all of these considerations have been subordinated to the flowing, ornamental rhythm of the overall composition.

Degas, who supported and collected Gauguin, bought the picture in February 1895 at the Drouot auction.

14   *Vahine no te Vi (Woman with a Mango)*   1892

72.2 x 44.5 cm

Baltimore Museum of Art

The question of the title has been linked to Gauguin's own description of a Tahitian wedding in *Noa Noa* and with Pierre Loti's novel *Le mariage de Loti* (1879). The girl in front seems to be in quest of a man, the girl behind (though she may only be a second image of the same girl) to have asked the question while making the hand gesture or *mudra* of Buddha as teacher. In this case, the subject is two stages in an initiation into love. Possibly there is a connection with the small figures in the background at left. Gauguin made repeated use of the decorative motif of a crouching woman; she seems to have been borrowed from the right-hand harem lady in *The Woman of Algiers,* which Eugène Delacroix painted in 1832, at the highlight of his North African travels, sixty years before Gauguin went to the South Seas. Delacroix was prompted to grant glowing colors their own autonomous values, and his admirer Gauguin was to repeat this.

15 *Nafea faa ipoipo? (When will you marry?)* 1892

101.5 X 77.5 cm

Rudolf Staechelin Family Foundation, Basel

As so often, Christian and Polynesian ideas are merged in this painting. And as so often with the syncretistic Gauguin, an interpretation in unambiguous terms is impossible.

The woman standing has been done after a medieval Eve and, covering her genitals, represents the Fall of the first humans in Paradise, here lushly tropical. However, the *varua ino* of the title is a wicked demon who frightens Tahitians when he appears. His piercing eyes in this painting glitter in a masklike face. No doubt he is also the tempting devil of the Old Testament.

16   *Parau na te varua ino (Words of the Devil)*   1892

91.7 x 68.5 cm

National Gallery of Art, Washington

17   *Two Tahitian Women on the Beach*   1892

91 x 64 cm

Academy of Arts, Honolulu

An inverted Oceanic version of Edouard Manet's *Olympia*, which Gauguin had copied in February 1891 shortly before departing for the South Seas. The artist made ampler comment on this than on any of his other works. An incident which is described as a nighttime scene with Tehura in *Noa Noa* acquires a second perspective in a letter of commentary written to Mette in December 1892:

"A kanaka girl is lying on her stomach, her frightened face partly visible. She is lying on a bed spread with a blue *paréo* and a light chrome yellow sheet. A purplish violet background with a scattering of flowers like sparks of electricity; beside the bed is a rather curious figure. . . .

"What is a kanaka girl doing lying completely naked on the bed in this somewhat risqué position? Waiting for love! That is true to her nature, but it is indecent and I will not have it. Sleep! That would imply that the act of love was over, which is still indecent. All I can see is fear. What kind of fear? . . .

"The *tupapaù* (spirit of the dead) suits this picture. For the kanaka he represents constant fear. . . . Once I have hit upon my *tupapaù* I give him my whole attention and evolve the subject of my painting from him. The nude is only secondary. . . .

"What can a ghost mean to a kanaka girl? She has no knowledge of theatre, and if she thinks of a dead person she inevitably thinks of someone she has already seen. So my ghost cannot be anyone but some nice little woman. She is stretching out her hands as if to seize a prey. A sense of the decorative prompts me to adorn the background with flowers. They are the flowers of the *tupapaù*, phosphorescent, a sign that the spirit is giving you his attention.

"Tahitian belief—the title, *Manao tupapaù*, has two meanings:

"To think

"To believe/ghost

"Either she is thinking of the ghost.

"Or the ghost is thinking of her."

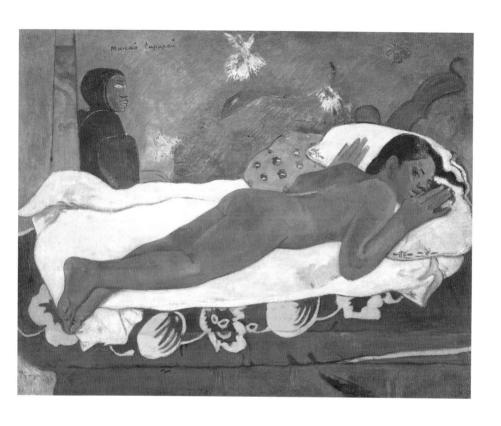

18   *Manaò tupapaù (The Spirit of the Dead Keeps Watch)*   1892

73 × 92 cm

Albright-Knox Art Gallery, Buffalo (N.Y.)

In Moerenhout and Bovis, Gauguin had read of the Arioi sect, who practiced free love. It was a hierarchical sect, and members saw themselves as apostles of the god Oro. The god was said to have founded the sect when, attracted by the beauty of Vairaumati, he descended to earth. This is the episode Gauguin has chosen. We see Vairaumati sitting completely naked in an ancient Egyptian pose on a *paréo,* smoking a cigarette with an ironic air. There is fruit on a table beside her, and to the right behind her, cropped in a manner inspired by Japanese graphic art, stands the god in a position of meditation. The two idols farther to the left are products of Gauguin's imagination, of the kind he carved in wood at the time. In another version, instead of a sophisticated cigarette Vairaumati is holding a coconut seed as a symbol of the son conceived by Oro.

This anecdote does not accord with the actual handed-down version, which states that the first Arioi was a chief of Raiatea chosen by Oro.

19 *Vairaumati tei oa (Her Name is Vairaumati)* 1892

91 x 68 cm

Hermitage, St. Petersburg

"I saw trees that no botanist would recognize, animals whose existence was unsuspected by Cuvier, and people only you could have created."

August Strindberg's description of Gauguin's art seems perfect for *Te nave nave fenua*. Taking considerable liberties, it transposes the temptation of Eve to a Tahitian paradise. Instead of a serpent (there are no snakes on the island), Satan here is a winged lizard, which Odilon Redon's lithographs may have prompted Gauguin to. A flower, likewise a product of the imagination, has replaced the apple tree (unknown on Tahiti). Eve herself is immense, with the features of Teha'amana, who supposedly had seven toes on one foot—an anatomical anomaly that appears in the painting.

20 *Te nave nave fenua (Delicious Land)* 1892

89.5 × 72.1 cm

Ohara Museum of Art, Kurashiki (Japan)

D espite the title, there seems to be no rivalry between the two women, who are not talking. Rather, the question might be directed at those who would see the painting in the future and might envy Gauguin and his models their tropical *dolce far niente*. The seated woman is borrowed from a kneeling figure on the frieze at the Theatre of Dionysus in Athens, a photograph of which Gauguin had in his possession. Delacroix, seeing the white-garbed Arabs in Morocco, had already felt that classical Greece could be remet in more primitive peoples. The headband of flowers worn by the profile figure is reminiscent of an ancient laurel wreath.

The reclining woman may have been added later. The two bodies, bright but shadowed, stand out against the rosy lilac sand. All trace of realism has been abandoned in favour of color harmonies; the line of the strand caresses the women's bodies; and the reflections in the water are a vibrant, abstract pattern, intoxicating in its glowing brightness.

21 *Aha oe feii? (What, are you jealous?)* 1892

68 x 92 cm

Pushkin Museum, Moscow

The hairstyles, gestures, patterns on the fabrics, body lines, and waves are all organized into a decorative, Japanese-style pattern of surfaces characteristic of *art nouveau*.

22 *Tahitian Women on the Beach* 1892

110 x 89 cm

Robert Lehman Collection, New York

Gauguin's surroundings at Mateiea, transformed somewhat into a paradise, the bounty of nature epitomized in the mango tree at center. On the green shoreline path in the foreground, a horseman and a walker are going their separate ways. The hut at right may perhaps have been Gauguin's own.

23   *Fatata te moua (By the Mountainside)*   1892

67 x 91 cm

Hermitage, St. Petersburg

"On one side was the sea; on the other, the mountain, a deeply fissured mountain; an enormous cleft closed by a huge mango leaning against the rocks.

"Between the mountain and the sea stood my hut, made of the wood of the bourao tree. Close to the hut in which I dwelled was another, the *faré amu* (hut for eating). . . .

"On the purple soil long serpentine leaves of a metallic yellow make me think of a mysterious sacred writing of the ancient Orient. They distinctly form the sacred word of Oceanian origin, ATUA (God)."

Thus the painter's description in *Noa Noa* of his surroundings at Mateiea. The hut he lived in is in the middle of this picture. The landscape is a luxuriant carpet of bright colors. In *Diverses choses,* Gauguin recorded these thoughts on the visual rhythms and non-representational attraction of carpets: "It only remains to speak of color from an artistic standpoint. Pure color as the language of the listening eye, its evocative power. The Orientals, Persians and others have done the most in developing the vocabulary of this language of the listening eye. They have endowed their carpets with a wonderful eloquence. Painters—if you are looking for a color technique, study those carpets: there you will all find instruction—color determined solely by its own appeal, not fixed by the definition of things perceived in nature."

24   *Matamoe (Landscape with Peacocks)*   1892
115 x 86 cm
Pushkin Museum, Moscow

In the spirit of classical painting, Gauguin was here imagining the rituals of the ancient Maori as a pastoral idyll. A tree divides the scene symmetrically; beyond, a mountain screens off the outside world. In the middle distance at left, girls are dancing in worship of an idol that recalls a colossal Egyptian Memnon. Two women in white are seated in the foreground at right, the cross-legged one apparently listening to the flute player.

George Forster heard music of this kind too, though his assessment of it was governed by eighteenth-century Europe's concept of harmony:

"One of the young men had a flute made of a bamboo, which had but three holes; he blew it with his nostrils, whilst another accompanied him with the voice. The whole music, both vocal and instrumental, consisted of three or four notes, which were between half and quarter notes, being neither whole tones nor semi-tones. The effect of these notes, without variety or order, was only a kind of drowsy hum, which could not indeed hurt the ear by its discordant sounds, but made no pleasing impression on our minds."

25   *Mata mua (Olden Times)*   1892

93 X 72 cm

Thyssen-Bornemisza Collection, Lugano

26   *Arearea (Pastimes)*   1892

75 x 94 cm

Musée d'Orsay, Paris

In a letter Gauguin referred to the painting as an "old tapestry." Instead of spatial depth it uses vertical layering. The colored shapes give an impression of having been cut out and assembled in inlay work. The seated woman is playing a reed flute. In *Noa Noa* Gauguin associated the instrument with night, and perhaps also with the moon goddess, Hina:

"But the rays of the moon play through the bamboo reeds, standing equidistant from each other before my hut, and reach even to my bed. And these regular intervals of light suggest a musical instrument to me—the reed-pipe of the ancients, which was familiar to the Maori, and is called *vivo* by them. The moon and the bamboo reeds made it assume an exaggerated form—an instrument that remained silent throughout the day, but that at night by grace of the moon calls forth in the memory of the dreamer well-loved melodies."

The young woman in white is carrying a basket of gardenia flowers. In the foreground at left is a jar decorated in the Marquesas style, and beside it a dog, its attention apparently fixed like the girl's on something happening beyond the scene before us.

In 1895 in Paris, Gauguin was asked about his seemingly unnatural use of colors. Gauguin responded with his definition of an art like music, divorced from reality, a definition which seems well suited to paintings such as *Pastorales Tahitiennes:*

"And what of your red dogs and pink skies?"

"Absolutely intentional and necessary. My whole work is calculated, carefully considered. It is music, if you like to think of it that way! Using the pretext of a theme taken from life or nature, I arrange lines and colors to compose symphonies, harmonies, that represent absolutely no reality at all in the banal sense, nor express ideas directly, though they do inspire thought as music does, not by means of ideas or images but purely through mysterious affinities our brains sense with such arrangements of colors and lines."

27   *Tahitian Pastoral*   1892

87.5 x 113.7 cm

Hermitage, St. Petersburg

The athletically built Tahitian woman at right has a touch of the hermaphrodite in her austere facial features and severe physique; feminine traits accompany the masculine in her. She anticipates the ceramic sculpture *Oviri* which Gauguin made in 1894 during his last stay in Paris. The picture, though, lacks the dimension of murderous cruelty. *Oviri* means savage, and Gauguin took the word as a pseudonym, using it for his writings. Here Teha'amana is still seen stroking the animal at her lap, a puppy dog or wolf, which the foreboding clay goddess will subsequently trample underfoot.

28   *E Haere oe i hia? (Where are you going?)*   1892

96 x 69 cm

Staatsgalerie, Stuttgart

"In this square, where all are equal and all are mixed, one witnesses scenes of indescribable realism. Everything is offered and everything bought. It is a market of love, or rather, as it is so picturesquely called there, a market of flesh.

"These market scenes inspired one of Gauguin's best known paintings, *Ta matete* (the seemingly Tahitian title is in fact a corruption of the English word *market*). The highly stylized picture shows Tahitian girls of pleasure in the foreground, wearing their best dresses. They are sitting on a bench waiting for customers, while behind them two men stripped to the waist are carrying large tunny fish on poles to the indoor market.

"Resourceful experts have identified in the bearing and gestures of the women a quite different source: a group of Egyptian courtesans. It is on a sarcophagus fresco of the XVIII dynasty, from Thebes, now in the British Museum in London. Gauguin had taken a photograph of it with him to Tahiti."

Bengt Danielsson, *Gauguin à Tahiti et aux îles Marquises.*

TA MATETE

P. Gauguin

29   *Ta matete (The Market)*   1892

73 x 91.5 cm

Kunstmuseum, Basel

This painting relates to the Maori cult of the dead, which died out in the late nineteenth-century; Gauguin added features of various cultures to it. The idol on the mound may represent Taaora, the creator of earth. The fence below with the death's-heads is of Far Eastern origin. The original appearance of burial sites of this kind, of which Gauguin only found remains, was described by George Forster in his *Voyage round the World*:

"[The place was] an uncultivated projecting point, where different kinds of plants grew in wild luxuriance among several sorts of shrubs. On coming out of the shrubbery they saw a building of stones, in form of the frustum of a pyramid; the base might measure about twenty yards in front, and the whole consisted of several terraces or steps above each other, which were ruinous and overgrown with grasses and shrubs, especially on the back or inland part. This the native said was a burying-place and place of worship, *marai*, and distinguished it by the name of *marai no-Aheatua*, the burying-place of Aheatua, the present king of Tiarroboo. Around it were placed perpendicularly, or nearly so, fifteen slender pieces of wood, some about eighteen feet long, in which six or eight diminutive human figures of a rude unnatural shape were carved, standing above each other, male or female promiscuously, yet so that the uppermost was always a male. All these figures faced the sea, and perfectly resembled some which are carved on the sterns of their canoes, and which they call *e-tee*. Beyond the marai they saw a kind of thatch erected on four posts, before which a lattice of sticks was placed in the ground, hung with bananas and coconuts *no t'Eatua*, 'for the Divinity.'"

30 *Parahi te marae (The Sacred Mountain)* 1892

68 x 91 cm

Philadelphia Museum of Art

"Tahitian girls with satin skin and loose, wavy hair, a copper complexion that goes wonderfully with the dark green of the island."

Matisse in a letter to his wife, 1930

31   *Ed Haere ia oe? (Where are you going?)*   1893
91 X 72 cm
Hermitage, St. Petersburg

This formal portrait, painted in March 1893 before he returned to France, seems to have been Gauguin's farewell to his lover and model, Teha'amana. She is wearing her loveliest Paris dress, has put flowers in her hair, and is holding a plaited palm fan like a scepter. The title of the painting alludes to the Tahitian custom of entrusting children into the keeping of the extended family, since all the island's inhabitants were traditionally said to have sprung from the union of Hina (matter) and Taaora (spirit). Gauguin partly owed his knowledge of Polynesian mythology to the tales Teha'amana had told him. For that reason, presumably, he portrayed Hina on the frieze behind her. She resembles Parvati, the wife of the Hindu god Shiva. Above Hina there are mysterious hieroglyphs not unlike the sole surviving Polynesian written symbols found in 1864 on Easter Island and shown in Paris at the 1889 World Fair, In Tahiti there were one or two tablets of script of this kind, which Gauguin must have been familiar with. These hieroglyphs, however, do not match any of the writings that have been found. The fact that he introduced this still-undeciphered script into the painting surely suggests that the mentality of the island people, rooted as it was in a distant past, ultimately remained inaccessible to him. This very enigmatic quality constituted part of Teha'amana's attraction for Gauguin.

32   *Merahi metua no Teha'amana (The Ancestors of Teha'amana)*   1893

76.3 x 54.3 cm

The Art Institute of Chicago

This generously composed picture, structured economically using only a few colors, conveys that sense of the permanent with which Gauguin was possessed on Tahiti. The sweeping terrain and the recurring curving lines are typical Gauguin features. Here, the painter seems as much at one with nature as the man in the foreground carrying fruit.

33   *Tahitian Landscape*   1893

68 x 92 cm

Institute of art (The Julius C. Eliel Memorial Fund), Minneapolis

The god Fatu, whose bust is seen at top right, is associated with the earth in Tahitian legend. Gauguin borrowed this tradition for his writing on Polynesian religion, which he titled *Ancien culte mahorie*. In it, the subject of this picture is described in terms that refer to Moerenhout. Hina says to Fatu: "Bring people back to life after their deaths." Fatu answers: "No, I will not awaken them to life. The earth will die, the vegetation will die, so let human kind who live off them die too." — "Do as you please, but I shall see to it that the moon is born again."

In Paris in 1894–95, Gauguin made ceramic, plaster, and bronze masks modeled on Fatu's features. The picture was reproduced on the cover of the Durand-Ruel exhibition catalog in 1893, and was bought by Degas.

34   *Hina Tefatou (The Moon and the Earth)*   1893
112 x 62 cm
Museum of Modern Art (Lillie P. Bliss Collection), New York

A nude viewed from behind, in the manner of Degas's women at their ablutions. "Never have I seen more beautifully built or stronger men and women," Matisse wrote to his wife in 1930. "One cannot imagine the skin color of these Oceanian people. It is not copper, but red gold."

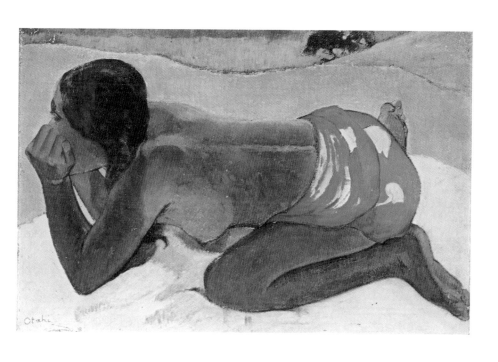

35   *Otahi (Alone)*   1893

50 x 73 cm

Private collection

In *Noa Noa* Gauguin tells of a trip to the interior of the country: "Suddenly, at an abrupt turn, I saw a naked young girl leaning against a projecting rock. She was caressing it with both hands, rather than using it as a support. She was drinking from a spring which in silence trickled from a great height among the rocks.

"After she had finished drinking, she let go of the rock, caught the water in both hands, and let it run down between her breasts. Then, though I had not made the slightest sound, she lowered her head like a timid antelope which instinctively scents danger and peered toward the thicket where I remained motionless. My look did not meet hers. Scarcely had she seen me, than she plunged below the surface, uttering the word, *Taëhaë* (furious).

"Quickly I looked into the river—no one, nothing—only an enormous eel which wound in and out among the small stones at the bottom."

Though the girl in the painting is clothed, and is raising her eyes to an apparition above her, there is at least a notional link with the text and the experience behind it. Generally speaking, Ingres' *The Spring* may be seen as the inspiration for this picture. More specifically, Gauguin was prompted by a photograph taken in 1889 by Charles Spitz and showing an island native amidst lush vegetation drinking at a rock spring, the water from which is falling into a pool as in this work.

36   *Papa moe (Mysterious Water)*   1893

99 x 73 cm

Private collection

Women resting on a roofed-over veranda and the shaded grass during the heat of the day. One of them is ironing while the others are doing nothing. They are all native women, but their clothing is European, loose-fitting mission dresses or colorfully printed fabrics, as if in a colonial fashion magazine; the foreground figure, so inimitably casual in pose, seems particularly reminiscent of such magazines.

Though undated, the picture was probably painted in 1891–92, when Gauguin was taking an active interest in his everyday surroundings. Pierre Bonnard's art took up scenes of this type after 1910. The spatial composition of this painting, using the posts and the perspective-drawn veranda boards, is especially clearly defined.

37   *Siesta*   1893

87 x 116 cm

Philadelphia Museum of Art (Mr. and Mrs. Walter Annenberg Collection)

Chronology

1848 June 7: Eugène Henri Paul Gauguin is born in Paris, the son of Republican editor. Clovis Gauguin. His mother, Aline Marie Chazal, is the daughter of painter and lithographer André François Chazal.

1849 August 8: After Louis Napoléon's coup d'état, the parents leave France with Paul and his sister. During the voyage to Lima (Peru) the father dies at Port Famine (southern Chile).

1855 Return from Lima.

1859 Paul attends the Petit Séminaire de la Chapelle Saint-Mesmin in Orléans and later the Lyceum in Paris.

1865 Paul becomes a cadet helmsman in the merchant navy. Voyages on the *Luzitano* between Le Havre and Rio de Janeiro. In late 1866 he sets off for thirteen months' sailing around the world as a sublieutenant on the *Chilli.*

1868 March: Joins the navy as ordinary seaman, second class.

1871 Discharged from military service. Apprenticeship in stockbroking to Bertin, a Paris banker. Gauguin begins to paint in his free time.

1873 November 22: Marries Mette Sophie Gad, a twenty-three-year-old Danish woman. Five children are born: Emile, 1874; Aline, 1876; Clovis, 1881; Jean René, 1882; Pola, 1883.

1874 At the home of his guardian, Gustave Arosa, Gauguin meets the "father of Impressionism," Camille Pissarro. Together with his colleague Claude-Emile Schuffenecker he takes painting lessons at Colarossi's, a private art academy.

1876 First exhibition at the Salon, together with Carolus Duran, Meissonier, and Gérôme.

1877–78 Still working at the stock exchange, Gauguin paints on the banks of the Seine and at Pontoise, where he frequently meets Pissarro. They becomes friends as master and pupil.

1879 Shows work at the Fourth Impressionist Exhibition at 10, rue des Pyramides, Paris (and in 1880, 1881, 1882, and 1886 too).

1881 Gauguin meets Cézanne. Following a sojourn in Brittany he exhibits a number of Pissarro-influenced paintings at the Salon.

1883 After the collapse of the Union Générale, Gauguin quits his job as a stockbroker to devote himself to art. He becomes poor. Breach with Cézanne.

1884 Moves with his family to Rouen, and in October to Mette's parents' in Copenhagen.

1885 Returns to Paris with Clovis. Mette remains behind in Copenhagen with the other children.

1886 Important artistic turning point at Pont-Aven in Brittany, from Impressionism to the decorative surfaces of Cloisonnism. In August he meets eighteen-year-old Emile Bernard, who admires him greatly. Late in the year he becomes friends with Theo and Vincent van Gogh in Montmartre, Paris. Meets Degas.

1887 With his friend Charles Laval he travels to Panama, where he works as a navvy on the building of the canal. In June he travels on to Martinique. Discovers tropical landscape.

1888 In spring returns to Pont-Aven. In summer his work with Emile Bernard produces synthetic Symbolism. From October to December, unwell, he is in Arles at the invitation of Vincent van Gogh. The two artists quarrel badly and at times violently, finally parting.

1889 In early May, Gauguin exhibits seventeen paintings done in Brittany, Arles, and on Martinique at Café Volpini during the Paris World's Fair. He then goes to Pont-Aven again, and in the autumn on to Le Pouldu.

1890 Return to Paris. Friendship with Symbolist writers and artists: Redon, Mallarmé, Monfreid. Gauguin's influence on young painters such as Denis, Sérusier, and Bonnard increases.

1891 February 23: An auction of his work is held at Hôtel Drouot, raising only a modest 9,860 francs. June 9: Gauguin arrives at Papeete (Tahiti).

1893 Return to Paris. Inherits a small legacy in September. During his stay in France he writes his autobiographical memoir of Tahiti, *Noa Noa,* together with Charles Morice.

1894 In the spring he goes to Le Pouldu in Brittany and then to Pont-Aven.

1895 February 18: Auction of his work at Hôtel Drouot, without significant result. Second Tahiti journey. November: Settles at Punaania, twelve kilometers south of Papeete.

1897 In April he learns of the death of his daughter. *Noa Noa* is published, illustrated with colored woodcuts. Attempts suicide during the Christmas period.

1899 Edits two satirical magazines: *Le Sourire* and *Les Guêpes.*

1901 September 10: Moves to Atuana on Dominique in the Marquesas Islands.

1903 May 8: Dies at Atuana.

Selected Bibliography

Anderson, W. *Gauguin's Paradise Lost*. London, 1972.

Bodelsen, Merete. "Gauguin and the Marquesan Gods," *Gazette des Beaux-Arts,* vol. 6, no. 57 (March 1961), pp. 167–80.

Cachin, Françoise. *Gauguin*. Paris, 1968, 1988.

Danielsson, Bengt. *Gauguin à Tahiti et aux îles Marquises*. Papeete, 1975.

Dorival, Bernard. *Le carnet de Tahiti*. Paris, 1954.

Fezzi, Elda, and Fiorella Minervino. *Noa Noa e il primo viaggio a Tahiti di Gauguin*. Milan, 1974.

Field, Richard S. "Gauguin's Noa Noa Suite," *Burlington Magazine,* vol. 110, no. 768 (September 1968), pp. 500–511.

————. *Paul Gauguin: Monotypes*. Philadelphia, 1973.

————. *Paul Gauguin. The Paintings of the First Trip to Tahiti*. Cambridge, Mass., 1963; New York and London, 1977.

Gauguin, Paul. *Ancien culte mahorie* (begun in 1893). Facsimile edition, edited by René Huyghe. Paris, 1951.

————. *Correspondance*. Edited by Victor Merlhès. Vol. 1 (1873–1888), Paris, 1984; vol. 2 in preparation.

————. *Lettres à Georges-Daniel de Monfreid*. Edited by A. Joly-Segalen, with an essay by Victor Segalen. Paris, 1918, rev. ed. Paris, 1950.

————. *Lettres à sa femme et ses amis*. Edited by Maurice Malingue. Paris, 1946.

————. *Noa Noa* (1893–1897). Translated by O. F. Theis. New York, 1919 (reprinted 1985).

————. *Oviri. Ecrits d'un sauvage*. Edited by David Guérin. Paris, 1974.

Gauguin. Catalog of the exhibition in Washington, Chicago, and Paris, 1988–89.

Gray, Christopher. *Sculpture and Ceramics of Paul Gauguin*. Baltimore, 1963; New York, 1980.

Guérin, Marcel. *L'Oeuvre gravé de Gauguin*. Paris, 1927; rev. ed. San Francisco, 1980.

Howarth, D. *Tahiti: A Paradise Lost*. London, 1983.

Kornfeld, Eberhard, Joachim Harold, and Elizabeth Morgan. *Paul Gauguin: Catalogue Raisonné of His Prints*. Berne, 1988.

Monfreid, Daniel de. "Sur Paul Gauguin," *L'Ermitage,* vol. 3 (December 1903), pp. 265–83).

Morice, Charles. *Gauguin.* Paris, 1919.

Pickvance, Ronald. *The Drawings of Gauguin.* London, 1970.

Rotonchamp, Jean de. *Paul Gauguin.* Weimar, 1906.

Teilhet-Fisk, Jehanne. *Paradise Reviewed: An Interpretation of Gauguin's Polynesian Symbolism.* Los Angeles, 1975; Ann Arbor, Mich., 1983.

Thomson, Belinda. *Gauguin.* London, 1987.

Wadley, N. *Noa Noa: Gauguin's Tahiti.* Oxford, 1985.

Wildenstein, Georges. *Gauguin.* Vol. 1. Paris, 1964.

Picture Credits